More...

Life-Changing...

Life-Giving...

Never-Ending...

THOUGHTS...

To you...

With all my Love...

Copyright © 2016 by Soul T Alma
ISBN: 978-0-9969667-6-4

Other Creations

Books

- **Energies In My Body... The Greatest Blessings Of My Life!!!** (Amazon.com)
- **Energías En Mi Cuerpo... ¡¡¡Las Bendiciones Más Grandes De Mi Vida!!!** (Amazon.com)
- **Running Out Of Time... Is That Even Possible???** (Amazon.com)
- **Se Me Acaba El Tiempo... ¿¿¿De Verdad Crees Que Eso Es Posible???** (Amazon.com)
- **Más… PENSAMIENTOS… Transformadores… Que-Dan-Vida… Que-Nunca-Terminan…** (Amazon.com)

Websites

www.soultranslations.com

www.traduccionesdelalma.com

Contact Information

Email Address: SoulTAlma@yahoo.com

Contents

Do not think about page numbers or anything else... You will get there... Wherever "there" is... If and when it is the right time for you... All in perfect timing... Like they say... No worries... Only Joy!!!

Chapter 1-- Thoughts... Thoughts... And **More THOUGHTS...**

11:11-- Epilogue

Chapter 1--Thoughts... Thoughts... And More THOUGHTS...

Thoughts... Reflections... Messages... Sometimes caused by "interference" ... Sometimes caused by "false guidance" ... Understandings... Energy... Communications with Our Inner Self... With Our True Self... With Our Source... With Our Universe... What are they??? ... Where do they originate??? ...

Inner World/Relationships-2/14/14 @ 6:46 am

It is as if I always sensed... Even in my most confused times... That if it wasn't "like that" ... It didn't make sense to me...

Most of the relationships and couples of any kind that I saw and see in the world did/do not make any sense to me... To what I know... To who I Am... So that always created confusion and perhaps even false beliefs in me...

And at the same time I always had this clear image of "the way" it should be...

And when I said "like that" ... I meant "the way" I always Knew it should be for me... And not seeing any of "that" always caused great discordance inside of me... To the point of feeling that "not belonging" that I felt for such a long portion of my life...

Inner World-7/17/14 @ 5:15 am

Writing has become a form of meditation for me... (5/29/16-I have explained more on this in the book "<u>Energies In My Body... The Greatest Blessings Of My Life!!!</u>") ...

At specific points "something" accumulates in me... And I've come to know now that "I have to" sit down... Let it out... And write it...

I always resist it because I have no time... And because I know that most of the times when I sit down and start letting it "out" ... More and more comes... And something that at first would seem to only take "x" amount of time and energy, usually becomes 5 or 10 or 100 times more...

But even as I many times resist with all my being not to start... It continues to build up... Until I finally succumb to it... And then...

Then the most Fluid and Beautiful things come out of me... To the point that I am Always amazed when everything is "done" ...

And I Always end up reading it many, many times after I finish... "Not knowing" where it came from... Knowing it wasn't truly me... Or was it??? ...

But the most Beautiful happens when I finish... That sensation that I "have been" emptied inside... A Happy... Serene...

Secure... Joyful Feeling... Ready for what Life brings :) ...

Inner World-7/17/14 @ 5:43 am

Song "Where dreams begin" (official Disney video) ... Playing in the background... A collage video that my child has of songs from different cartoons, etc... I absolutely Love that song!!! ...

https://www.youtube.com/watch?v=fY5JMeVkUGE ...

And this phrase "Just put your hand in mine... And then we'll go where dreams begin" kept playing back in my mind... In my body... In my Whole Being...

But... Really... Where is that??? ... Where do Dreams begin??? ...

In Love... In Knowing (truly KNOWING) OneSelf... And Trusting the "knock on the door" from Within... In Knowing we are connected to Our Pure Essence... To our

Guidance... To the Universe... In Believing in "Magic"... In letting OneSelf flow... But having taken the time to Purify our "Inside" ... To know the Truest Essence of OurSelves... Otherwise, we may follow "false guidance" ... But when we have Purified ourselves from all interference... Then we can Trust and follow our Impulses blindly...

Where is that??? ... Where do Dreams begin??? ...

In not forcing or controlling... But Allowing... Following Impulses... And Trusting... Especially Trusting that We are part of "A Whole" ... And when We are Purely In Sync with That Whole... Everything develops/takes place perfectly... In Joy and Harmony...

[Interference=things that cause our Total Body to be unbalanced=negative thoughts, negative emotions, false beliefs (especially the ones given to us by other people), false feelings of love that are used to manipulate us through partialized stories, through partialized music/songs to manipulate us without us even realizing, fear, guilt, inadequate foods, inadequate habits, etc]

Relationships-7/17/14

People "jump" from one relationship to the next without taking time to know themselves...

To "heal" themselves...

To purify or "empty" themselves out... Of interferences...

Or perhaps to "fill" themselves up... With Love (Pure Love)...

So they can be ready to receive and give more Love... And the most important... To know themselves at a deeper level and know what they want...

We are constantly changing...

We always need to know ourselves again and again...

Our perspectives and desires from that moment of our lives are not the same ones as the ones from the previous moment... Or the following moment...

It is as if people always have the need to have somebody (AnyBody) to be able to "live" (or to "suffer")... Incorporating more and more interferences and toxins in the process... Getting farther away from ThemSelves...

Without realizing that first... And more important than anything else... They have to identify with Their Self 100%, to be able to Love ThemSelves... To be able to have Self-Love...

Only that way they will be able to truly Love someone else...

Anyone else.

Inner World/Relationships-7/17/14 @ 3:00 pm

"Honeymoon with The Universe"... I said this to a friend of mine in a conversation over the phone, and afterwards I realized that this was truly a message for me...

I have been in this state for over a year now (5/28/16- and at this point for over 3.5 years)... And the purpose has been to Know MySelf... To understand the signs... To understand and refine my ways of communicating with My Universe... With My Source...

Many people leave one relationship and go right away to the next...

I have never been able to do that... Even in my most disoriented times... But in all the previous occasions when I have been by myself, I have been in suffering... In depression...

Without truly understanding the Beauty and the Value of being alone and Going Within...

I have been in a "victim mode" ...

Without understanding the endless wealth that we find when we go WithIn... Without fear... And "All The Way" ... Endlessly...

Spirituality-7/20/14 (Continued on July 16th and July 23rd of 2016)

The way I imagine/see/Feel our "Physical" and "Non-Physical" "States Of Being" is just like the states of matter... Especially the three most known/visible ones from our standpoint here in our physical world... Yes, of course I am referring to solid, liquid, and gas...

And every time, since all these processes started to take place in me from the very beginning of 2013, many images... Very vivid "images" started to happen inside of me...

In this particular case I am referring to images related specifically to that: my "States Of Being" ...

And it was something so Magical and Beautiful to me...

And so very interesting...

They were not really images... They were things I... I truly cannot find a way to explain it through words... They were not things I saw/see in my mind, NO...

I Felt/Feel them in My Body...

But the way I had been feeling things in my body during all my life up to that point had been extremely superficial and almost imperceptible, if I compare it to the way I have been Feeling "things" in and through My Body from the very first CLEAR moment back in January of 2013, when all these Beautiful, and many times scary and unbearable, Processes started to happen in me... (See "_Energies In My Body... The Greatest Blessings Of My Life!!!_")...

And among the "things" I have been Feeling... (I wanted to use the adjectives profoundly or deeply or viscerally or extremely or... But truly... None of them accurately reflect the way I have been Feeling "things" in My Body since then) ...

It is as if the body has become something totally different compared to what it used to be...

Probably many of the people reading this will think I perhaps lost my mind... But nothing like that :) ...

During all of what I have Lived In and With My Body these three and a half years I can tell you that it is not just "a body" anymore... No...

I feel IT IS a Tremendous Intelligence...

The key is to learn to tune to it...

And understand the way it communicates with us...

And follow... No, is not really "follow", but Be one with It...

Embrace It...

LOVE IT...

Honestly, I have come to understand and Feel My Body as an Intelligence that is able to Perceive Subtle important things...

An Intelligence that is most (ALL) the time more intelligent than the brain and the mind...

And now that I am writing about it, a clear Understanding came to me...

The reason I Feel that The Body is an Intelligence more Intelligent than the brain and the mind is because throughout the first 42 years of my life, and even in the last four, I have constantly realized that the brain and the mind are very easily influenced by the external world and can many (most of the) times give us false guidance, distorted messages, false understandings...

And so far I have never ever experienced that with My Body since all this started to happen in me from 2013 on...

No...

It is as if The Body were an internal Intelligence that is totally isolated from the outside world in the sense that it is not influenced by it to give you false guidance...

And at the same time it is so Purely In Tune to it, that it is capable of guiding YOU in YOUR world in a very Clear and Unbiased/Unaltered way...

But because it is so Sensitive to "what is coming in from the outside in so many different ways" (everything that comes either directly inside the body in the form of food, etc, or what comes in through the interpretations that the mind makes of the things that happen in our outside world), The Body can/will almost shut down, as a "survival mechanism," if not in the presence of Purity…

Yes!!! …

That is exactly what I experienced all my life up to "that point" in 2013…

It is becoming SO ABSOLUTELY CLEAR now!!! …

For all of what I have described before to happen Purely, The Body needs to be Pure… Free of what I call interferences: toxic foods and drinks, toxic feelings and emotions and thoughts, toxic conversations and news, etc, etc… And yes, even, <u>and especially,</u> toxic sexual and sensual experiences…

That is YOUR job…

To treat and respect Your Body the way it deserves to be treated and respected...

It is something so unbelievable, but so Magical and Beautiful at the same time!!! ...

And deep within myself I feel bad for the way I mistreated My Body during the first 42 years of my life...

But at the same time I Know this is all part of the Beautiful Process of me Becoming one with Me...

Of me Becoming All-Of-ME...

And I Know that perhaps this (the extreme to what my body became -the level of numbness- from being so mistreated, and the stark difference to the way it started to become when my desperation levels took me in the path of starting to do some things to purify my body and somehow be able to continue to exist in it) is precisely what has allowed me to Clearly Sense/Perceive/Feel all the signs and signals it started to give me back in 2013 and that have continued until now...

It is something like...

In a room full of different fragrances you cannot Perceive the Subtle Essences... But in a totally odorless one you can Perceive even The Most Subtle Essence of all...

Or...

In a place full of noise coming from everywhere one cannot perceive a Beautiful Subtle Note, but in Silence...

Oh, in Silence!!! ...

In Silence you are able to Sense and Feel The Universe, The Infinite, The Eternity...

You are able to Perceive It ALL Inside of YOU...

And the same way that in these three and a half years I have come to Clearly and very Intensely Feel MyPhysicalBody like I never thought was even possible... In that same manner I have come to Feel the "NonPhysicalMe" ...

And that "NonPhysicalMe" has been something so new to me... Even though I somewhat felt its presence all my life...

But I always thought "it" was something else...

Something external...

Something that was not part of me...

Not Me...

And something that I did not even dare to mention to anybody because I knew they would probably think I was out of my mind...

How could that be??? ...

That was impossible!!! ...

If it was not something physical/tangible/material...

If it wasn't something that could be "moved from here to there" ...

Or picked up...

Or at least touched...

And if one could always feel its presence...

Then... Oh... Then...

Then it was probably something that belonged in the group of the "strange and scary things" that is better not to even talk about...

But now that I am writing about all of this... That is exactly how I also felt my physical body during the first 42 years of my life anyways...

Exactly like that...

Like something that I did not really totally feel and/or understand...

Like it wasn't really me...

Exactly like something that also belonged in the group of the "strange and scary things" that is better not to even talk about...

I guess this is why getting to Sense and Feel MyPhysicalBody the way I have started to Sense and Feel and Communicate with IT since the beginning of 2013 has been as Beautiful and Magical as getting to Sense and Feel and Communicate with TheNonPhysicalMe...

This is probably why I have so clearly and vividly felt, since all of this started to happen in me, from January of 2013 on... That <u>I was getting to Know Me... For the first time ever!!!</u> ...

And this is such a Beautiful experience... I truly never imagined something like that could even be possible...

And the level/degree in which I was perceiving/interpreting things as they were happening in me during these three and a half years is nothing compared to the way I now so Profoundly Understand everything that has happened In Me...

Now that I am able to see the Whole Picture, it is all very Clear...

And it is a Beautiful Picture...

Something that I hope everyone gets to experience in This Lifetime...

And the sense of Calmness....

The sense of Perfection...

The sense of Belonging...

Finally a sense of Belonging To and Perfection Of...

Life...

This World...

Me!!! ...

So, I Clearly Know now that I got to Meet and Truly Know

ThePhysicalAndNotPhysicalMe both at the same time...

And I think this is why at "that same time," I was able to feel in My Body the clear "image" of the transition between My States Of Being (Physical and Non-Physical) as something very perfectly similar to the transition between the states of matter...

And it has been very clear to me how in some cases this transition...

This communication...

This Blending between My States Of Being happens in a very easy manner...

While it is very difficult...

And even "impossible" in many other cases...

Yes...

Probably that is exactly what was happening during the first 42 years of my life...

That this communication...

Even this knowledge...

Or even the awareness that they (my States Of Being and the "communication/transition" between them) existed...

And the meaning that they have...

Was something totally impossible for me to sense...

But...

Why??? ...

Why was it something so impossible for such a long time??? ...

And why even now...

After all these Knowings and these Understandings...

After everything that has taken place in me during these recent years...

Why after all of that this blending/communication between ThePhysicalAndNonPhysicalMe seems to be weaker or even almost non-existent sometimes? ...

And the more I feel all this in me...

The more I realize that it all goes back to that extreme sensitivity that OurWholeBody has to both Our External and Internal Worlds...

And to the level of Purity in which we live...

And yes...

The "easiness" of the transition between our Physical and Non-Physical States Of Being is very similar to the easiness of the transition between the states of some matter compared to the other types of matter...

And for some types of matter that transition happens very easily under "normal" everyday conditions...

For some other types of matter a great deal of "effort" (change in temperature and/or pressure, etc) is required for the transition to take place under the same "normal" everyday conditions, even if for only a short period of time...

And for other types of matter this transition cannot happen at all under the common types of effort that we can apply (extreme changes in temperature and/or pressure) in our regular everyday lives...

    And sometimes we are so rigid...

    So "hard" ...

    So stiff inside and outside of us...

    So full of toxic things we put inside our Bodies and our Souls in every imaginable way (through foods, drinks, news, conversations, sexual/sensual activities, etc, etc)...

    So full of negativity...

    So full of fear...

    Of doubt...

    Of lack of Love...

    That there is a very "strong... visible... hard" boundary between the physical part of us and that other part that some of us sense that is there but we cannot quite understand...

Such a hard and stiff boundary within OurSelves...

That even applying all the effort we can possibly apply cannot facilitate that Communication...

That Blending...

That "Transition" ...

Between Our Physical and NonPhysical Selves...

Or to even be aware of the degree and the importance of their Existence...

And in that case (which happens in at least 90% of us at this point)...

The only possible way is to slowly...

With great deal of Love (even if at first we do not even realize it is Love)...

Purify OurSelves from all of that "toxicity" ...

From all of those "interferences" ...

To then Slowly...

And Beautifully...

Start experiencing the Magic of those little discoveries...

Of that Transition...

Of that Communication...

Of that Understanding...

Until one day there has been enough "Purifying" of OurSelves to allow a major "Event/Process" (something similar to what had started to happen in me since "That Day" of January of 2013)...

And especially, and most importantly, for us to have enough clarity in OurSelves to be able to perceive "it" and allow "it" to happen/unfold within OurSelves (See "_Energies In My Body... The Greatest Blessings Of My Life!!!_") ...

Now... 8/8/2016... As I was driving a few minutes ago... For some reason all these things I have been writing about the Physical and NonPhysicalMe have come to me once more...

And again... "Things" don't come really to my mind anymore... Except the everyday routines, such as: "should I go to the supermarket first or to the Post Office first" ... Or anything else along those lines... But those other "THINGS" go directly to my Body...

At the beginning of all of these processes to start to happen in me back in 2013... I always felt all these thoughts and feelings and "things" came to me "from somewhere else" ... "Out of the Blue" ...

Back then they always felt like coming "from above" ... Always from above... As if they were imposed on me... As if they entered in me from that "above" place... As if I did not have anything to do with any of that...

And then eventually that "above-place" was not so obvious... I still felt that all of "that" came from somewhere outside of me... But not exactly "from above" ... It was from everywhere... From "places" that felt much closer to me...   And now... I would say since the last three months or so... Nothing feels outside of me anymore... I feel everything originates WithInMySelf... The routine everyday thoughts and decisions... And those other THINGS: Thoughts, Messages, Guidance, Impulses... Not sure how to call them...

But I clearly feel that those "routine-ones" come more from my mind... And those other "Sudden, Deep, Life-Changing, Sometimes-Absurd, Always-Extremely-Meaningful Things" come from My Body... I can clearly Feel them in every particle of My Being... It is as if "That-Something" that was before always outside of me is now always InsideOfMe... But I can still clearly feel the two...

Anyways... I almost forgot to write about what "came to/from My Body" while I was driving :) ...

It is the remembrance... Or the understanding... Again, words fall very short to describe all of this...

But right after all of this started to happen to and in me back in 2013... I would say for about the first year, or a year and a half, I always felt somewhat like I was floating... Like I was less dense... Something perhaps similar to those people that are shown walking on the moon...

I was not much in my body... I was not in my mind... I wasn't inside of me the way I was used to being all my life, so attached to the surface... Not sure how to say it...

This was so new to me... I did not know what was happening... Like I explained in "*Energies In My Body... The Greatest Blessings Of My Life!!!*" ...

I just had the sense that I needed to let it happen and go through whatever I was going through... (But knowing what I know now, I KNOW that I really didn't have a choice... Even if I had tried to stop it, I would not have been able to) ...

And I guess that feeling... That sense of not being inside my body... Or anywhere specifically, for that matter... Allowed me to "go through all of this" without losing my mind and losing myself in the process...

Going back to the analogies I was mentioning before about the similarities between My States Of Being and the states of matter... I can clearly feel that the way I existed the first 42 years of my life was pretty much like "a solid" ... Or like something that was "trapped" in a solid...

But then when all of this began in me... Within that first year and a half... I can clearly feel now that I went to the other extreme...

That is why I felt I was not inside my body or my mind... And I was in that "floating-like" state...

I can see clearly now that in that analogy I lived in a gas-like state in that year and a half...

And it was so "extreme" to me because I feel there was no evident transition for me...

It was like going straight from a solid to a gas, without transitioning through the liquid phase...

Something very similar to sublimation...

After that year and a half it was more like coming back to me... But never again to that rigid solid state...

And during the last three months I feel clearly I have been in a liquid-like state... Very "fluid" ... Very "easy-going" ... Very HAPPY... And "things" do come up... But when they do, I am able to go around them... Or let them go through and out of me... Or I am able to go through them and out of them... In a much easier way... In a much shorter period of time... And every single time, I am able to deeply feel the Wisdom in whatever it is that may be taking place in MyWorld... Especially in MyInnerWorld... At any given moment...

Now I am easily able to be in the "solid state" and back... And in the "gaseous state" and back... Very easily... In the everyday conditions of our everyday world... And it is a Very Beautiful Thing!!! ...

****

Many of the images that came to me... From the very beginning of all of this happening to me back in 2013... Use water as an analogy for different things I was sensing about my "State Of Being" at different points of this process...

And lately I have encountered different examples of other people using water to illustrate similar things...

And, of course, the reason is so obvious to me!!!

Water is something we have all experienced since we were born into this world... It is the most abundant substance in our world, as far as we know :) ... It is fairly safe in its most common "way of being" ... And especially, it is something that is easily experienced in the three states of matter known to all of us, under the conditions (specifically temperature and pressure) of this world...

Inner World-7/26/14

I had noticed that several times lately I had "jokingly" asked my closest friends, if I sensed they were in a somewhat "out-of-balance" state: "Are you stressed out?" ...

I really did not make anything out of it... It just caught my attention as some type of pattern that I was not sure why was taking place...

But one day I mentioned something similar to a very close friend back then and she suddenly said: "What are you talking about? ... That I am stressed? ... You should look and see because I have noticed that you think everyone is stressed out, but maybe you are the one that feels that way" ...

And that was a very loud wake up call for me...

Something similar to if they had thrown a bucket full of iced water on me...

See... I had been feeling so happy and eager and relaxed and clear minded after having gone through these processes for a year and a half now... Compared to how I had felt all my life prior to 2013...

But this made me "go within and realize" that even though I thought that I had reached some type of existential state that was being very elevated... I was very... Very far from such a state...

Now... 7/28/16... Almost two years later than when I began to write these thoughts... I can understand everything much clearer...

Of course back in 2014... After having lived a year of going through those processes that started in January of 2013... Of course I felt at such optimal state of being...

Of course!!! .... After living the first 42 years of my life in such numbness... Depression... Negativity... Lack of belonging to anything I saw around (or even felt inside) of me...

After living in such disorientation and such fog for so long... It is perfectly understandable that living such a Magical and Out of the Blue life-changing experience... I would feel like I've finally arrived some place...

And when my friend made that comment I suddenly realized that she was right on...

That was exactly what I had been sensing lately that made me feel a little "strange" ...

And I was not able to recognize it because in my mind it was not possible that I was going to go from such a Bright and Magical state to the depths of the numbness I had lived all the time before...

And even though I did realize that I had been stressed out about things... And that I was not in that "idyllic" state of being in which I thought I was... I wasn't anywhere near all that negativity in which I had lived almost all my life...

Now... Having lived Life two more years after I started writing these thoughts... And over three and a half years after these processes started to happen in me...

After all this I realize that "those moments" are going to continue to happen again and again...

I also know that they are there for very specific reasons... But I will never go back to that purposelessness.... That lack of self-esteem... And ultimately... That lack of self-love in which I was living before...

And I realize that perhaps in any of the previous times of my life something like this would have caused me to take a dip in that "quicksand" that is so well known to me...

And then from there have other experiences and other feelings and other emotions that would cause me to take an even deeper "dip" in "it"...

And then another...

And another...

And not be able to grab "the wheel of me" and guide my attention...

And my feelings...

And my body...

And my emotions...

And my Heart...

To observe and interpret and act and react to whatever was happening inside and around me in a more meaningful way...

Or, to say it accurately...

Not to allow me to feel and sense the "guidance" that "that-other-less-attached-to-this-world-by-the-five-senses-and-therefore-having-more-aerial-view-part-of-me" was trying to give me...

Blocking my connection with Me...

Blocking my connection with Love...

Not letting Me be/exist freely inside of me...

Not letting me be the Love that I am...

Not letting me feel Me...

Becoming more and more depressed...
More and more pessimistic...
More and more negative every time...
But I also realize that one of the main differences now is that I can see what is happening...
I can see my reaction...
I can feel my feelings...
And I automatically am able to grab "the wheel of me"...
And realize there is something behind "whatever it is that is happening to me at the moment"...
And then I am able to almost step outside my body and observe the situation... And observe me in the process...

Of course I still deeply feel things...
I am a very sensitive person...
But I have such a deep level of Understanding now...

Such a deep level of Self-Love…

Such a deep "level" of Love…

That "It" allows me to guide My Emotions…

My attention…

My Heart…

My Body…

In a way that allows me not to be so entangled in that mesh of everything that may be happening around and inside of me…

And then I quickly understand the Meaning…

Or the Understanding that is there for me…

Or the Love Message that is there…

Inside of me…

Behind… No, not behind… It is more accurate to say: Within "all of that" …

And once I reach that point it is as if a Love Explosion happens from Within MySelf…

And that Love Explosion and all that Process makes me live Something Magical...

Inner World/"Outer World"- Some time in the middle of 2014

I was feeling that "jumpy/bouncy/eager/supper-happy" inner state that I used to feel almost constantly back then... During the first year or two of this processes to start to happen in me... Then I started to notice those "bouncy moments" were decreasing in frequency and intensity and now (7/28/16) I have not felt them that much in the last couple of months... And now that I write about this... One would think that if I am not feeling that bouncy, eager, super-joyful, jumpy inner state... Then I should be feeling in a similar way to what I used to feel the first 42 years of my life... But... No... Nothing like that... I predominantly feel calm... Clear... Relaxed... Happy... And even in the moments when I feel "less than that" ... It is nothing at all compared to the way I used to feel before... I do not reach such deep "levels of despair" or those other "levels of numbness" ... And I am able to get back out of "any-level-of-whatever-I'm-in" much sooner...

Anyways... I so clearly remember that incident, sometime in 2014... I cut through a neighborhood where I never ever go... I never ever take that route... I was bouncing off out of happiness... And I think that intense feeling of "happiness for no reason" was what made me explore a new route... Windows rolled down... Music in my car to the max (which is not that loud, really)... Singing... My arm hanging on the side... Tapping on the door to the rhythm of the music... Suddenly I see that a policeman started to drive behind me... Without passing me... For a long long time... And I continued my behaviors... I was just "super happy for no reason"... Nothing wrong with that... I hope everyone could feel like that on a regular basis... It would truly be a Very-Happy-World...

I now think that the fact that I was so super-bouncy-happy was what caused him to focus on me... And then the fact that I stayed like that for so long made him continue to pay attention to me... And there was nothing for me to worry... I was just happy... Everything else was fine... BUT... I did not realize that my birthday had passed two days ago... And I had forgotten to put the new sticker on my plate... I was living in a floating-like state back then... And I was stopped... And I received a ticket... And all of a sudden all that happiness shrunk... Got to the "0" point... And then went to the negative side where I felt... Not sure exactly how to call it... I think "sadness" would accurately summarize it... I truly did not feel angry or anything... I think I was just astonished... I truly could not believe that something like that could happen in the middle of such Happiness... But now, 8/29/16, as I revisit this moment, I can clearly see that it was not a "normal state" for me yet... I was just so super-bouncy-happy in contrast to all the numbness and all the negativity I was used to feeling during my whole entire life up to 2013... But I was not stable in it yet... That is probably why all those "coincidences" happened one after the other to culminate at that point... And the way I handled and processed all of it within myself... And the way I interpreted it... And what I got out of it showed me that even though I was not "stable" in that "New State of Being" yet... I was very far from the way I used to be all those first 42 years of my life...

Now, 8/29/16, I have not been in that "super-bouncy-happy-joyful-state" for about the last four months... I feel more stable... More used to it... I see all of this is my normal way of Being now :)

Blockages/Inner World/"Outer World"- 8/31/14

While I was meditating... I know that my doctorate is the biggest blockage I have in my life right now... I mentally set time for it... I don't do it...

But that time is mentally blocked... And I do not move on with other things either...

I am closed up to love... To friendships... Etc... Because I am reserving "that time"... "That energy" ... To devote it to finishing my doctorate...

But I don't do anything...

And I feel even worse...

And "punish" myself even more by criticizing me...

By feeling guilty or inadequate in some way... Because that way my life will continue to be out of balance...

Even when I am involved in many perfect beautiful relationships with family and friends... I am still closed to my creativity and flow because I have my time and my mind and my energy "blocked (reserved)" for finishing my doctorate... But I don't do it...

I realize that my True Energy is not there anymore...

That is something I started too long ago...

When my True Energy was 100% there...

But I don't use my time or my mind or my True Energy now for anything else either because I am "blocking" them for the sole purpose of finishing my doctorate...

As a result I am totally stuck...

My time is stuck...

My mind is stuck...

My True Energy is stuck and blocked...

Closed to the things I truly want to do and be involved with at this "Now Point" of my life...

Conclusion... And my Whole Being is telling me a whole different conclusion... But I am forcing this to be my now-conclusion...

I should use every available minute and bit of energy in my life to finish my doctorate...

To GET OVER with it...

And then finally be able to move on...

To Flow...

To Be FREE :) ...

In LOVE ...

And JOY :) ...

****

(Continued on August 28, 2016) ... And like that I continued for another whole year... Suffering through life... Trying to finish... Finding Hope... Finding something within this process that truly interested me... And I finally found it... And the possible venue to do it appeared in my path as if by Magic... But my life circumstances at the moment really were not allowing me to focus much on this and finally be able to finish... So I was deeply suffering... And on July 27, 2015 I received a letter saying I had been dismissed from the program... Something I had feared during the last 7 years of my life... And I was not able to just let go... Not me... I was always able to very successfully complete all my studies... Oh no... Not me!!! ... I was not going to be the one to give up on this!!! ... And "Life" found a way to take it away from me... Just like that... And it has been one of the most relieving moments of my life... And I have never looked back to this... No regrets... No shame... No guilt... Pure calmness... And a deep relief!!! ...

Inner World-12/10/14

I Love my life...

I Love my Journey...

I Love this Beautiful unfolding...

Steady...

Slow...

Surprising...

Delighting... :)

Inner World-4/29/15

In one of those Astrology predictions/descriptions that I read sometimes, they said that My Sign equals possessions, and Venus means receptivity, receive, owning...

And I started to reflect on the fact that I have been exactly the opposite to that...

I have been very "low-deserving" ...

Always blocking my abundance...

Especially in the financial and professional areas...

But also in the flow of Love, etc...

They also mentioned "Gather... and then, when you have enough, you can give away" ...

And now I am just thinking... This has been so difficult for me... Even though I consciously say "I am going to do this and start to change in those areas" ... But nothing happens and I end up in the same situation...

Could it be that that's what I came here to learn? ...

And they even went on to mention that specifically on my birth-day there was a special code of abundance-meter high... And they mentioned the terms "Empowerment... Manifestation... Transformation... Strength... Opening to change... Rely on inner sources for answers... Strengthen what is authentic... Transform what is not real to you... Idea...

Creating my authentic message through Joy... Stable... Magnetic attraction... Stay true to your values... True to what fulfills you to the core... The importance of rest, so the brain is fresh and your Energy flows...
Communicating your voice with integrity... Through the depths of your Soul... Merging mind and heart" ...
    I LOVE MY LIFE!!! ...

Inner World-6/24/15
    My ingrained beliefs when I was little... Always thought I was wrong... Different than the rest of the world... Now, energetically/spiritually speaking, I can understand each and every one of those "ingrained beliefs" ... And Know the reason for them...

Relationships-6/24/15 @ 3:30 pm
    Today... Talking to my dad...

My dad said something about a relative's relationships that made me kind of puzzled because that comment did not really have anything to do with what we were talking about…

It was something that was "placed" in the middle of the conversation apparently "out of NoWhere" …

And I kept prodding him to try to find out the connection…

And dad goes "Well… At least when they live together they will not be alone… It's not easy to be alone" …

And I go "Well dad, I do not know what to tell you, I have been alone all this time and I am the happiest I have ever been… I have never felt lonely… However, I have felt very lonely when I have lived with somebody… Apparently "not alone," like you say" …

Dad: Oh yes… I know… It's better to be alone than in the wrong company…

Me: No dad... It's much more than that... And I don't even want to tell you because if I say this to the majority of people, they will look at me as if I am out of my mind... And I was truly trying to stop the conversation right there... But I felt "That Push"... It was something more powerful than me... And even though I paused, "that something" picked up strength again and pushed me to keep going... "Well, dad, it is not even just in relationships... It is everywhere... Energetically... Chemically... If one wants to be the most Stable State... Pure... Balanced... One cannot find that other than within OneSelf... Energetically... Chemically... Any-way-you-want speaking... The minute you introduce other "things" ... Even just one other... "That" alters the Balance... The Equilibrium... The Purity" ...

Dad: Yes... You are right...

Me: So... I agree that people should want to be in relationships... But it should be for other reasons... To stir life... To have fun... To add spice... I am not sure... But not just "not to be alone" ...

So that conversation ended there... But it has kept on going on and on inside of Me for hours now...

And more thoughts have come to mind...

1) Feeling full... Complete... Balanced... Whole with and within OneSelf... And then share the Joy of our Whole-Being with another...

2) Yes... It is true that many, many people, desperately need to be with another... Not only in intimate love relationships... But in general... They feel lonely... They feel emptiness inside... They feel out of balance...

And the images of chemistry, physics, the environment, music, etc, have come to mind again…

Chemistry- Unstable "entities" with a vacant electron, etc… NEED something that "completes" them to "feel" they are balanced…

Physics- High pressure/low pressure… It goes from one to the other for balance… And it can, in extreme cases, end up in a hurricane, etc…

Environment- When one species is removed from it… For whatever reason… It causes a lack of balance… That niche may then be easily taken by a "non-native," "non-natural" species… And this would cause an "apparent" balance… But it is 99.99% of the times harmful to that environment…

In all these examples there is some type of lack…

Of instability…

And that sense of balance and completion that one feels in union with the other is usually not a True one…

Or a meaningful and beneficial and lasting one…

And this goes way beyond to even all those affiliations that people get involved into… Needing to belong to something that controls and guides them… Perhaps that is why I never had any inclination to be anyone's boss or supervisor or guide… Because I always had this Knowing… Even as a small child… We need to be balanced in A Whole first… Then share Our Whole with Another Whole… And then expand and grow from there… Perhaps transforming into something else together…

6/25/15 @ 4:25pm

So... After more of this conversation expanding inside of Me... I now understand... "Finally!!!" ... That relationships are the most important thing in life...

Even though I have perhaps spent my life trying to convince myself that one can be totally alone and still feel whole...

Complete...

Fulfilled...

That is not true because even if one could be by oneself in a deserted island there would still be relationships...

With the surroundings...

The air... The land... The water...

The plants...

The sun... The moon...

Etc... Etc... With OneSelf...

Even though I have always tried to explain to myself that one can live without love relationships... I realize this is not truly possible...

It is probably possible to live without a partner...

And that is as long as that Magnetic Pull doesn't happen...

That Magnetic Pull that really has nothing to do with just physical everyday attraction...

It is something Infinitely Beyond and Deeper and More Intense and Complete and Life-Giving and True-Love-Flowing than that!!!
...

But even when I have lived some periods of my life trying to be something similar to a hermit... I have still had many love relationships going...

It wasn't intimate physical love...

But it was Love anyways...

With my close relatives...

With those few others that somehow managed to be such a match to how I was feeling at those stages of my life, that I couldn't really keep them apart, even though I tried…

With those whom we need to interact with…

For longer periods due to work… Or childcare reasons… Etc…

Or short periods of time… A clerk at a bank or a store… Etc…

And in all those relationships…

Even the least seemingly meaningful ones…

Emotions are involved…

Feelings are involved…

Love is involved…

And all of them serve a very specific purpose…

The purpose of triggering…

Of waking something up inside of us…

Like a spark...

And that spark makes us realize about what we prefer...

Whether we liked this action, event, etc, through the type of emotion/feeling that that spark triggered in us...

Or whether we disliked it...

And from there we...

Sometimes automatically...

Or sometimes very consciously...

"Do" something about it...

Take some type of action...

Transform our attitude somehow in one way or another...

Now... 7/5/15 @ 5:47 am... As I was reading this again... It has just occurred to me that attitude is intrinsically related to our inner vibration (our "State Of Being" at that moment) and what we emanate...

Or maybe they are not just intrinsically related... But they are pretty much the same thing??? ...

Perhaps this is why that saying says "Attitude is everything" ...

Change direction sometimes...

Strengthen our push in the same direction we were going in others...

But in every case we are growing...

We are changing...

We are evolving...

And for most of us that means that during the first period of our lives we "evolve" opposite to the direction of OurTrueSelf...

Confused by so many interactions...

So many feelings...

So many emotions...

So many different expectations from everyone...

So much "interference" ...

But at some point...

It really doesn't matter when...

We feel the "Ultimate Pull"...

Usually it happens at that point in our lives when we are "stretched-beyond-our-limit" ...

Like a rubber band...

So "stretched-beyond-our-limit" that we have no other choice...

Either bounce back to reconnect to our True Self while we are still in "This Body" ...

Or totally break the connection with our Own Body, which is what keeps us able to enjoy life in this world...

Either way we will reconnect with our True Self...

And at that point when we bounce back we realize that it is All So Meaningful!!! ...

That all those years of stretching away from our True Self have been so important because they made us grow...

They made us experience life...

They made us know OurSelves more and more through all our interactions with others and with ourselves...

They made us understand what Life is... What Love is...

They made us Evolve and Become...

So... Yes... After all these "years" in This World, I have come to the total understanding of why some say that we cannot even exist without others...

Everything is so Interesting...

And so Beautiful...

And so Simple...

There is so much to Enjoy in this journey called Life!!!! ...

Have Fun along Every Step of The Way!!! ...

It Is ALL Worth It!!!!

6/26/15--- 6:55 am

Happiness is...

The things...

E-V-E-R-Y-Thing...

We take for granted...

But it usually takes most people losing them before they realize it...

Relationships-6/26/15 @ 7:25 am

Reflecting on "someone I know" ... As I see her coming back with someone else... And in this case I am just referring to "another friend" or "another relative" ... Cannot understand people's need to be with people all the time...

And everyone telling me to go out and be with someone... Etc... Etc... And "coincidently" right at this moment -5/28/16 @ 8:00 am- the song "November Rain" by Guns and Roses is playing...

Precisely the very last part that says "everybody needs somebody" ...

Do coincidences really exist??? ...

What are they??? ...

They are too "co-incidental" to be just what people lightly call "coincidences" :) ...

And even me...

Sometimes...

Thinking I am wrong... Or something is wrong with me because I do not act like everyone else...

For being in this "bell jar" ...

Almost isolated from the world...

Picking and choosing carefully...

So I can be in my "Purest State" ...

But I do not do it "on purpose/consciously" ... It just happens like that... I cannot do or be otherwise... I am not able to force myself to act differently...

Could it be that all this is part of "The Process" ... So I can allow everything to flow to me Purely... From wherever it is flowing? ...

Inner World-6/26/15

I have realized that the more it flows and I write... The more and more it flows... The key is for me to actually sit down and allow it to begin :) ... That's all!!! ...

Inner World-6/28/5 @ 1:05 pm

Before...

I didn't even allow me to realize I had Dreams...

Or Feelings...

Or Sensations...

Now...

Now <u>I Know</u> All Things Are Possible :)

...

Inner/Outer Worlds-6/30/15.

In the first 42 years of my life I've had a tendency to addictions ("dependences") ... Depression... Food... People... Etc...

Could it be that now I am addicted to exercise to keep me balanced? ...

Or to this State Of Being 100% "me with Me" maybe??? ...

Still grabbing on to something "external" ...

Still not totally whole/balanced within myself ...

Or is it that perhaps it will always be that way... Since both our inner and outer worlds are constantly changing? ...

Is it that we always need that "tool kit" full of those things that work for us to help us keep that balance? ... To help us "manage/understand" OurSelves in This Body in This World? ...

And that because both our inner and outer worlds are constantly changing... Even the contents of the "toolkit" have to constantly change in order to keep being useful to us? ...

Perhaps is it that we need to start seeing all of this as part of Life and part of our process to grow and evolve and expand and adapt and adjust and find the balance needed to assess our situation at each moment and focus on the direction we need to go next... Both InWardly and OutWardly? ...

Inner/Outer Worlds-7/1/15

We... People... Have the huge tendency to want to "live in herds" ... Always seeking to be with others... Not realizing that "it" is exactly what prevents us from becoming/aligning-with OurTrueSelf because of the huge amount of interferences "it" creates...

Inner/Outer Worlds

Sometimes "things" come to me in moments when I am very... Very busy... Or in a hurry... If I don't take a minute and write "them" down... "They" go and even when I apply great effort... "They" don't come back again... And I know they were very important "things"...

Inner/Outer Worlds-7/12/15 @ 8:47 am

When I focus too much... Trying to cause the thoughts... The feelings in my body... Etc... To flow through me... Not much happens...

But when I'm "focused" on something else... Or "unfocused" really... Because that "other thing" does not require my attention 100% ... Then many things flow and flow... And cause "waves of goose bumps" in me...

And I Know that those are the "things" I have to write somewhere... On whatever piece of paper... Because they tell me things... Because I was not forcing them to come to me with my mind... Because they came on their own... As if they had come "from somewhere else" ...

And afterwards I realize they are very significant "for something else" I still do not know "what for" at that time... Not yet...
It's like "they come to me" without me calling them... Without me "looking for" them... As if they did not come exactly from "inside" of me...

It is as if someone were "telling them" to me... Or as if "someone put them" inside of me...

And I can feel exactly the precise moment in which they were put inside of me... And then... Then I cannot stop writing until everything is totally "put" on "the paper" ...

Inner World/Outer World-7/16/15

So interesting how we "change" depending on who is perceiving us...

For example...

For the last couple of years I have consistently been a very "changed" person... Compared to how I used to be the prior thirty years of my life... I feel the best and the happiest I have ever consciously felt in all my life...

And yet... At any given moment in time...

I am a "different" person for different people...

One sees me and finds me very uplifting... Very beautiful... Very spiritual...

And the next second someone else has something to say in a somewhat critical way...

This is so intriguing and so very interesting to me...

I have been reflecting on this a lot lately and have realized that it all "works" in a way similar to a microscope...

The closer it gets to the "object" ... The more details...

The farther from the "object" ... The more general... The less details and therefore the less "friction" ...

Something very similar to what I mention in the book "*Energies In My Body... The Greatest Blessings Of My Life!!!*" (Chapter 7) ...

Usually the closer we are to the person... The more critical and hard and harsh the person is to us... And the more uncomfortable it makes us feel many times...

And yet... These are the exact people that we love and they love us the most... But they are the most difficult ones to deal with (both ways) ...

And it is that they love us... And we love them so much... That we/they would not want anything bad/displeasing to happen to them/us...

Not an event...

Not an action...

Not even a feeling…

Not even a thought…

We want to protect them so much that we act that way towards them…

They want to protect us so much, that they act that way towards us…

We love them so much that we react very deeply to what they say/do…

And vice versa…

And this can be very detrimental to any relationship in the end…

Some ties are pretty much unbreakable…

Regardless of the situation…

But some (like marriages, friendships, etc) cannot survive the intensity of this type of interaction…

And they break apart…

And even looking at it from the physics standpoint... It is perfectly understandable...

When two objects (people, in this case) are more distant apart (acquaintances, by-passers, distant friends) ... The interactions are weaker... Nothing affects much... The "negativities" do not impact as much... The love is not as intense... So this connections can stay pretty much the same way forever...

No one feels the need... Or the right... To interfere or have opinions or "change" the other one... In these types of "distant connections" the people involved are much more "accepting" of the others as they are... Much more unconditional... Should we say... love? ... Is involved... Yes... Definitely... Love...

But we, humans, are brought to this world "wrapped" around...

Or wrapped by...

Our five...
Or more...
Senses...
And we need and desire to feel more...
So those distant relationships are satisfying in their own way...
But we need more...

So even though we have stages in life when we decide we need to get away from it all and become some type of "cave-person"... And put distance between us and everything and everyone else... That cannot last forever...
And even if we do not feel the need... Or have the opportunity... To get closer to our own family or previous relationships... We make new ones...
And as we get closer...
The attraction gets stronger...

And that is the "honeymoon" phase (whether they are love or friendship relationships) …

But also…

Like what happens when using a magnifying glass…

They start seeing the imperfections in us more…

We start seeing the imperfections in them more…

And we start wanting to change them more and vice versa…

Or what they do or say hurts us more…

And in the process we evolve…

We grow…

We change…

Many times this change is for "the negative" …

Or…

To say it more precisely…

It is just part of the path that we need to follow to eventually become one with our True Self...

And we may become sad...

Shameful...

Regretful...

Depressed...

Or any other of the very "disconnected" feelings/states of being...

Or... In many other cases... We are at a stage in our lives when that interaction... That "change" ... Makes us be the closest to our True Self we have ever been...

And in both cases we can stick in that relationship forever (for the "good" or for the "bad") ...

Or... Like what happens in most cases...

For many different reasons that change our life circumstances...

Or for the plain and simple fact that we do not want to be with that person anymore...

That connection breaks apart...

And we continue the process of sailing through life...

Finding a place that attracts us... For whatever reason...

We live...

And we change...

And we continue...

And the key to life...

And one of the hardest things to do...

Is to see everything as "neutral"...

And to Love everything...

Even the experiences in our life...

People...

Things...

That we may perceive as bad or negative...

Because they helped us grow and expand by making us feel deep feelings (even if "negative") that helped us to know ourselves a little more clearly...

They helped us to define even more the things we would not want to have in our lives...

And the ones that made us feel the deepest Love...

Depths of Love we had no idea we were able to experience...

Helped us to know ourselves a little more too because they helped us to clarify who we are...

And to define a little more...

Or maybe know for the very first time...

What we love and want to incorporate in our lives...

And either way...

And in all the possibilities in between...

We come a little closer...

And a little closer...

To our True Selves (interferences out... Love in) ...

And then there are those times in our lives...
Many...
Many years for many people...
And the whole lifetime for many others...
When we see that year after year...
Event after event...
Person after person...
Are causing us to dive deeper and deeper into what we perceive as negative...
And we go down the hill of countless feelings that range from lack of self esteem to sadness to depression...
And end up even feeling that we do not belong in this world at all...
Like what happened to me during around thirty years of my life...

Until something happens…

Many times a very "sudden" …

Deep…

Impactful event…

Or sequence of events…

And perhaps the presence of a specific Being in our lives that throws us "in the arms" of our True Self…

Even if for a second…

And once we know that sensation…

That experience…

That feeling that has no parallel in the whole Universe…

There is no way we can ignore "It" …

And even when the "negativity" …

The busyness…

The "whatever" of our daily lives makes us get distanced from "THAT" again…

Eventually there will be another meaningful event…

Or person...

Or sequence of events...

That will put us "in the arms" ... (I do not say "face to face" because that is not enough... That is what we have been sensing all our lives and we see it as separate) ...

But in the moment when "that something" makes us fall in the embracing arms of our True Self (6/1/16--Which... In reality... Is US) again...

We get to know "It" a little more...

Sense "It" a little more...

Feel "It" a little more...

And there is no sensation or feeling in this Universe more deeply fulfilling than that...

And usually the more separated we have been... The more "impactful" that "encounter" with our True Self is... And sometimes even one chance is enough (if we are still in deep low self esteem only one chance may not be enough) ... So "enough" that we grab the wheel of our feelings and there is no way that we want to let ourselves go back to "where" we were before... And we are able to live life almost as one with our True Self...

And when the "frictions" of our daily interactions with ourselves and with the external world make us get away from "It" again... It is much easier for us to "grab the wheel of ourselves" and turn in the right direction...

In the direction of OurTrueSelves again...

And again...

And again...

Endlessly :) ...

Inner/Outer Worlds-7/21/15 @ 3:05 pm

Life is a journey...

No... But wait! ...

A journey is too big!!! ...

Feels too overwhelming!!! ...

Life is...

Life is...

Life Is...

The way we interpret and process... **A Split-Second** circumstance... Of both inner and outer worlds mixed together... At **Every Step Of The Journey**...

LOVE IT!!! ...

LIVE IT!!! ...

To The Fullest!!! ...

Inner World

Why does everything... Or almost everything... Flow to me in English? ...

Inner World/Outer World/Love/Abundance- 8/1/15 to 8/5/15

8/1-Went to "a city an hour away" to see "a cousin" that was in the hospital... I went there unannounced... And to see the expression of Joy... Surprise... And... Yes... Love... That emanated from Her Being is just priceless...   After I left there I went to see one of my few Best Friends... I had not seen him in 18 years... And we hugged and we talked and we cried together... Disregarding the thirty other people that were in the same place at that moment... And to feel the Joy... And... Yes... The Love... That emanated from both our Beings is just priceless...

8/2-Went to "a cousin's" house in my city... We went there to see "another cousin" that came with his family to visit from "a city an hour away" ... And as I was dancing with "that cousin" that came to visit from "a city an hour away" ... Whom I had not danced with... Or even interacted much with... In around twenty years... And no one else was dancing, by the way... The rest of the family was just sitting down and talking...

But I so wanted to dance "that type of music" with "that particular cousin" that came to visit from "a city an hour away" because I have never danced that type of music in such flow and harmony with anyone else in my life...

But as we were dancing just "that one" song... I tripped on a shoe... Did not think much about it at the moment... Continued dancing... Then stayed there talking and having a nice time with my family...

And I suddenly noticed the toe a little black... But thought it was because it was dirty from having tripped against the outside floor or something...

But when I got to my mom's house she said it was not looking good...

In all of that I never experienced the slightest negative feeling about anything... Did not feel sad... Or bad... Or regretful... Or shameful because it had happened...

Yes... I had a broken toe... But I was feeling so eagerly happy inside of me... To the point that I started to constantly ask myself whether I was crazy or what...

In any other previous time of my life I would have felt depressed and even desperate...

8/3-I woke up early in the morning... Around 3:00 am... Could not sleep anymore... There had been several days of wanting to finish writing and not being able to... Not because I did not have the time... But because I did not have the motivation... Or... Better yet... The Inspiration...

I could have motivated myself to do it... But after all of this that has happened to me for the last couple of years... (Explained in the book *"Energies In My Body... The Greatest*

Blessings Of My Life!!!") ... I do not want to motivate (or force) myself to do anything...

I just want to feel The Inspiration and ride on/with it to see where it takes me... So... Since I was not feeling That Inspiration... I could not get myself to do it... I did not want to do it like that... So I was just being patient with myself and flowing with it... Letting myself Just BE :) ...

But this morning I woke up so early... Eagerly got up... Eagerly sat at the computer and wrote... And wrote... And wrote... And so many Beautiful Things emerged from me... So beautiful!!! ...

I could not stop myself from writing... I knew there were things that were accumulated in me and that I wanted to write... And I started writing those... But all of a sudden all these other Beautiful Things started flowing and flowing and flowing...

I did not know where they were flowing from... I did not know why I was trying to write one thing and a different one was coming out... And I was trying to force myself to write what I wanted to... But that other thing kept on writing itself...

So... Having gone through that several times before... I quickly switched and let myself flow with what was coming from that place that is not exactly inside of me... But it certainly flows through me because I feel it very intensely... I know in this case I am serving as a canal or a pipe through which "that" flows...And that "that" feels as some type of energy or something similar...

I know I do not even have to ask myself what that "that" is...

I know without a doubt it is Love...

Pure...

Beautiful...

Love...

And I guess sometimes it does need a pipe or a canal to reach certain places... And I just Love it when I feel it flowing through me...

I Love it!!! ...

It is such a Magnificent sensation in my Whole Body...

In my mind...

In my emotions...

In my thoughts...

In my feelings...

In my spirituality...

I absolutely Love It!!! ...

So I wrote and wrote and wrote and I felt like I finished...

At that point I felt "that something" I know so well already...

That peaceful...

Calmed feeling...

That feeling of being complete...

Whole...

And I knew everything that needed to flow and be written in this particular case was done...

And I felt that Happiness...

That Relief...

That Joy that I have felt so many times before when I have written those many, many letters to THAT BEING...

Or the letters I have written to "those two other Beings" that I met in "that trip" ... (Explained in the book "*Energies In My Body... The Greatest Blessings Of My Life!!!*")
...

I Know all these sensations so well already!!! :) ...

<u>8/3</u>-Later that day I called "another cousin" to ask what I can do for the broken toe... But she was in "a city four hours away" ... In the middle of a flood... Trying to see how she could get out... Her so loved pet had died... We continued the conversation... I did

not want to mention my toe because what she had to say felt much more important to me... Then she said today was her mom's birthday... A Being I Adore so much!!! ... All of that happening the day I broke my toe... The day I felt so Happy and I was Inspired to write and write and write... And many things about Love and from Love flowed through me... So beautiful!!! ...

8/4-The idea/inspiration came to me that I am going to self publish in English... But I am going to make the translation to "my language" ... And if possible order only two printed copies... One for me... And the other one I am going to send to "The Wife" in that beautiful couple that I met in the trip to the "3.5-hr-away-country" as a gift... (Explained in the book *"Energies In My Body... The Greatest Blessings Of My Life!!!"*) ... It would be beautiful if I could be able to do that for her birthday... I understand the time between now and her birthday is too short... But if not... It does not matter...Whenever it happens it is going to be just perfect :) ...

<u>8/5</u>--Spoke a little to "those two Beautiful Beings" and my friend in that "3.5-hr-away-country"... With "The Husband" ... So beautiful!!! ... He was able to hear everything I said and the conversation was Beautiful and very fluid... Then spoke to "The Wife" ... Heart to heart... So honest... So "Soul to Soul" ... A conversation that lasted 1 hour and 58 minutes and some seconds altogether... And we did not even feel it... Time just flew!!! ... So much Abundance!!! ... So much Love!!! ...

<u>Inner World-11/10/15</u>

I want to live my life like A Feather... A Happy Feather... Going to all the exercise classes I Love... Being in nature at least an hour every day... Or... Better yet... As much as I want... Letting my creativity flow and materialize... In a financial abundance to do all the Beautiful things I Love to do :) ... Free-flowing...

Inner World-11/15/15

Do not stop writing... Or more precisely... Get on with it again... Take the time to jot down those "little notes" that occur to me... They... Sooner or later... Turn out to Be Precious "Messages" ... Precious Insights that came through me... For Me... Precisely and exactly FOR Me...

Energy-Inner World/Outer World-11/15/15

I heard someone talking about "emotional vampires" ... Or "energy vampires" ... I cannot remember exactly...

I can just remember "that visceral feeling" I felt... "Noooo!!! ... That is not accurate!!! ... Not accurate at all!!!" ...

I used to believe that too!!! ... I used to be "convinced" about it during the first 42 years of my life...

But in the end... In the Very Essential End it all comes down to the fact that WE are our ONLY "any-kind" vampires... Anything else is just our own excuse...

Or... Better yet... Anything else is part of our own journey...

Of that Beautiful Journey toward Self-Discovery...

That Precious Journey of becoming One with OurSelves through the Discovery of... The Embracing of... The Blending with... **Self-Love**... Through the recognition... Through getting to Consciously KNOW... That in the end... In the Very Essential End... And In the Beginning... And In Our Essence...

That is the only thing that exists… That is Who We Are… Nothing else… **Love**…

Inner World-1/2/16 @ 8:47 am

Take TIME OFF from everything… Not to go somewhere… But to Be With ME and let MY SOURCE… Let MY PUREST ESSENCE… Let LOVE flow through me… Just that…

Inner World/Outer World/The Importance Of Focus-2/16/16

I still…

And will Always…

Remember the day all I had in front of me was the darkest most closed sky I have ever seen…

For some reason I turned around… One-hundred-and-eighty-degrees around "my axis"…

And at the same instant…

From that the same spot...

I was suddenly immersed In The Most Beautiful Bright Sunset I have ever seen...

Inner World/Outer World-2/16/16 @ 4:25 am

I remember when I used to tell my parents: "But I didn't ask to come to this world!" ... Trying desperately to imply: "Accept me as I am!" ...
But during all those years I never fully and deeply realized of the fact that perhaps I was saying it to MySelf because even I could not accept me... Always pointing out the negative... The faults... Always seeing my "lacks" ... Always putting myself down for the most meaningless reasons...

"All We Need Is Love"-Inner World/Outer World-2/18/16 @ 3:24 am

One of my relative's phrase, when talking about the situation of the world: "Everything is done on purpose" …

My reflection… "NOOOO!!!! … Each one of us is a collection of all that existed before… Of all the human fears… Of the disproportionate lack of Love… Of so much "steamrolling" everyone in our paths… Especially… Consciously or not… Ourselves… Of so much "pretending" just to fit in a cast that does not fit us… A cast that is not nearly Who We Are… Of so much comparing ourselves to others… Our Bodies… Our Emotions… Our Souls…

And in the middle of everything that was "avalanching/surging" through me and from me in that infinitely short instant… The Beatles song "All you need is Love" came to My Being…

There is such a deep truth in that simple phrase...

The problem is that what people call love is not really Love...

Once we "let" IT in...

True Love...

That Beautiful Flow...

That Pure Energy...

That Clear and Subtle Essence...

Once we finally get to Know IT...

Nothing else can coexist with IT inside of us at the same time...

And it is the most Beautiful Feeling...

The Most Beautiful State Of Being in the Whole Universe!!! ...

Love-Inner World-April 2016

IT is There...

Yes!!! ...

Of course I am talking about Love!!! ...

We just need to let IT out (or In)...

Like the water that comes out of a faucet...
We do not "see" that it is there...
But when you open it...
Even if just a little bit...
It starts to come out of the faucet (or into our life) ...

Love...
We CANNOT see it...
We Feel IT...

And many times...
Eventually...
Even if you don't consciously "open it"
...
That water (Love) finds its way "out of the faucet and into your life" ...
And...
"Ironically" ...

This is usually "caused" by some type of "malfunction"...

Something that went "wrong"...

But it allows you to see that, despite everything, It didn't run out...

That It is/was/will always be There for whenever you need it...

For whenever you decide to let It in...

To allow It to come to you...

Silence...

Inner...

Outer...

In our thoughts...

Silence...

That is usually how It (Love) comes out of/into us...

Otherwise it is very difficult to "hear It"

...

Or to ever sense that It is There...

Belonging-Inner World-4/29/16

I wasn't "here" all those first 42 years of my life... And to be more "fair" I should say thirty of those years (not counting the first 12) ... But if it were for what I was truly feeling... I should count most of those first 12 years also as years "I wasn't here" ...

That's how it feels now...

Inner World-4/29/16

Through all of these moments/processes... Through everything that happened in me from the beginning of 2013 on... In a very surprising... Sudden... And instantaneous manner... I was able to "rewrite/redo" MySelf and my past... (But in reality I didn't "do" anything... Everything happened in a totally automatic and unstoppable way) ... I was able to

Consciously Know ME... The Total-Me... And that word is extremely important for everything... <u>Consciously</u>... That is The Key!!!
...

<u>Inner World-4/29/16</u>

Sometimes is "being here" wanting to "be there" all the time... In a kind of total confusion and not knowing what we want and how to understand our instincts and impulses...

Sometimes is true guidance from within to be able to change our path...

And in order to truly know/understand the difference, it is absolutely important to "Be One With Ourselves" ...

<u>My Body-Inner World-5/1/16</u>

During all these last 3 (almost 4) years I have felt that my body's role in my life totally changed... Before it was something that I pretty much took for granted... It was "just there"...

Back in 2013 I started noticing how it "started" to give me many signs... And I started to be more and more in tune with IT... Until it came to a point that I realized that my body "thinks" and guides me much more clearly than my brain...

Inner World-5/26/16 @ 7:34 pm

I never really wanted to get too involved in "physical life"... In the things others find so appealing... Dating... Facebook... Twitter... Crowded places... Strangers... Etc... Etc... And do not see the need... I do not even see the point of any of that... And I truly never understood the reason why...

Inner World/Outer World-5/27/16 @ 1:50 pm

I want to have time to create and to put in physical form what is already inside of me... For that I need to be READY... Have a pad and a pen with me at all times... Then I can create at each and every one of those "little times" I may have :) ...

Meditation-Inner World/Outer World-5/27/16 @ 4:10 pm

Haven't been able to meditate anymore in the last couple of years... It is as if meditation helped me in its moment... A moment that lasted many... Many years... It had a very specific purpose in my life...

Now, it is like I have too much eagerness and playfulness in me to be able to be still... It is as if now I meditate in many different ways... Exercising... Writing... Enjoying nature... Enjoying deep connections with people... It is as if now I want to constantly LIVE...   Be fully awake/involved/aware and appreciative most of the time (except in very specific cases) ...

Inner World/Outer World-5/27/16 @ 4:20 pm

Always stayed away from things that would "anchor" me too much...

My Body-Inner World/Outer World-5/27/16 @ 4:40 pm

My FIRM conviction not to do anything drastic to my body... Plastic surgery... Stomach surgery... Pills... Knee surgery... Doctors for depression... Lipo... Etc... Etc... Even in my most confused and disoriented times... Even seeing that the majority of the people "do it" ... Even when very knowledgeable people that love me a great deal would advise me otherwise...

HOME=SELF-LOVE-Inner World/Outer World-7/20/16 @ 10:05 am

Have you ever felt a yearning for Home?

Have you ever felt a sense of emptiness inside?

Have you ever felt you are missing something within?

Have you ever felt that sense of not belonging?

That sense that even if you are in the most beautiful place...

Surrounded by lovely people...

You still do not belong...

You still feel empty...

You still feel like you are searching for something...

I am talking to you... Yes... You!!! ...

Maybe it is that you have been placing your attention somewhere else and not where you really should...

You have probably been looking outward...

You probably have been missing the only place that you should really be focusing on...

That place...
That Beautiful Place...
Is Inside YourSelf...

If you have felt that no matter where you are...

No matter if you are inside your house...

You still have been yearning for Home all your life...

You probably have been looking for home outside of yourself...

You have been probably missing the only place where Home is...

Home is Inside of You...

Look Within…

Always…

There you will find all the Beauty…

All the Blessings…

All the Love…

The True…

The Infinite…

Love…

It may seem at first that there is nothing there…

It may seem that mostly what you find there are worries…

Sadness…

Emptiness…

"Ugliness and lack of value" …

Home is Inside of You….

In that Infinite Place…

Once you start going within…

Faithfully…

At first it may feel strange…

It will most likely feel very strange because you are not used to it…

All your life you have probably been used to "going/looking" outward…

All your life you probably have felt somehow inadequate…

And that feeling of not belonging…

That empty feeling inside…

Yes, I know…

It will probably (most likely) feel very strange…

You probably have been used to finding fault in you…

For one reason or another…

Fault instead of Love…

Fault instead of Beauty…

Lack instead of Abundance…

Yes...

Home is Inside of You...

There is no need to search more...

And once you Faithfully and Consciously start Going Within...

And once you keep Going Within...

Once you go beyond all of "that strangeness"...

All of "that negativity"...

Once you go beyond all of that...

You start seeing The Beauty...

You start feeling like you are entering an enchanted forest where you find Love...

And Love...

And Beauty...

And more Beauty...

And more Love...

Yes...

Once you go beyond that boundary…

And you start getting in the area where there is more Love and Beauty…

And less strangeness…

And less negativity…

Then… Oh then! …

You will want to go there more often…

Home…

Go Within…

More…

And More…

And More…

Until eventually you Understand EveryThing…

And the main thing you will Understand is that All you were missing…

All you were searching…

All you had been yearning for all your life is You…

You...

Home is inside of you... In Self Love...
And It is Infinite...
It is Endless...
It is Bottomless...
It is Beautiful...
It is Self-Love...
It is You...

YOU Are Home...
YOU are what you have been looking for All Your Life!!! ...
YOU...
YOU...
Yes YOU... The Real... The-Whole-YOU
Look WithIn YourSelf!!!

11:11-- Epilogue

∞ ∞ ∞

www.ingramcontent.com/pod-product-compliance
Lightning Source LLC
Chambersburg PA
CBHW020011050426
42450CB00005B/416